TWO WOMEN I

I want to be a better man because of their belief in me.

I dedicate this book to my grandmother, Lona and my wife, Jennifer.

God has truly blessed me with the love of these two strong, secure women. Each in their own unique way, they helped provide a moral compass for me to follow as well as embrace the values that keep me grounded.

Granny, thank you for raising me and teaching me right from wrong. Thank you for wanting me.

Jenny, you are my one true north. Thank you for being a loving mother to our four boys. Thank you for trusting me.

Both Granny and Jenny made a conscious decision to be a significant part of my life. Sometimes it's the family that we create that gives us the strongest bond. I would not be where I am today without their unwavering support of my dreams. I am forever grateful for their unconditional love.

Jack Fallon

" Look within and find God.
Look back and thank God.
Look forward and trust God.
Look around and serve God."

-Unknown

CONTENTS.

CHAPTER 1
Grateful

"*I will give thanks to the Lord with my whole heart; I will tell of all your wonderful deeds.*" (Psalm 9:1 NRSV)

<u>GRATEFUL.</u> Every day I wake up and think about how grateful I am for God's blessings, especially the blessing of being raised by my Grandmother Lona.

My childhood was anything but normal, with a very humble beginning. I am sure many of us wonder if anyone really knows what normal means these days. What I do know is that my early experiences shaped me in ways that I now realize are unique blessings. I believe if you really want to get to know someone, you need to learn about their childhood. It's too easy to make assumptions about someone based on what you currently see on the surface. Social media, image, and material possessions interfere with truly appreciating people for who they are and where they came from.

The Beginning

My story starts on May 21, 1972, at Bi-County Community Hospital in Warren, Michigan. My mom and dad were very young and unprepared to raise a baby on their own. Throughout my childhood, I was bounced around from one house to another, making me feel like I had many parents and many homes. I think I must have been the poster child for the famous African Proverb, "It takes a village to raise a child."

Fortunately, when I was eight years old, my Grandmother Lona, who was 56 at the time, invited me to live with her in East Detroit. It was 1980, the same year I met my birth father, Jack Sr. He had been living in Texas while serving in the U.S. Marine Corps. When he moved back to Michigan, he lived with Granny and me for a few years. He became a truck driver and spent a lot of time on the road. When he was home, it was nice to have the three of us together. He was only 16 years older than me, and some days he felt more like my older brother. I could tell that Granny enjoyed having her son and grandson live with her by the way she doted on us. She is one of those special people who enjoys taking care of others. I was grateful that one of them was me.

Granny Lona

Life with Granny

I vividly remember what it was like living with Granny because she always made me feel loved. She was caring and nurturing. For the first time, I felt a true sense of belonging. I remember waking up to the mouthwatering smell of Granny's pancakes, filling our home in the morning. They were my favorite. The stack she would put in front of me was so high, I could barely see over the top. They would be smothered with about a stick of butter and drenched with maple syrup. I can still taste them now.

Her laughter was like music that filled up our home.

Granny was an upbeat person and so much of a positive influence on me. Since my mom wasn't a big part of my childhood, Granny knew she needed to teach me right from wrong, to be respectful, and to be grateful. She was old school for sure. Like when she would say, "Jack, always mind your P's and Q's and stay away from bad things!" At the time, I didn't even know what my P's and Q's were, but I did know, by her tone, she was serious.

Granny was a stickler about being prompt. If I wanted a ride to school, I had to be ready and out the door before she got in the car. No kidding, there were times she left without me. She instilled in me that being on time meant being early. She believed that it showed respect for others.

I admired Granny for her beliefs and strong work ethic. She worked at Hudson's department store in downtown Detroit. She had a strong opinion that everyone needed three things: a good coat, a good pair of shoes, and a good bed. Granny worked hard to provide all three for me. This is just another thing, well, three things really, I am grateful for. I think she liked nice things in threes because she bought three Chevy Caprice Classic cars in a row: blue, silver, and black. I remember each time she drove home in her new car.

"Granny, it's the same car!"

"Well, Jack, it's a different color."

I'm not sure whether she was a creature of habit or simply loved the Classic.

She made me follow her rules and everyone else's rules too. Sometimes when I was misbehaving, Granny gave me the silent treatment to make me learn a lesson. This painful silence was the worst kind of punishment, but the worst moments hold the best lessons. Whenever this happened, I knew I had let her down. I can remember the times when she cooked dinner, and we ate without her saying a word to me. I would sit at the table looking right at her making funny faces trying to get her to smile, but she didn't budge. She was clearly in control. I did not like the silence. Granny knew she couldn't let a young boy run wild under her watch, and she was right.

Even though Granny was strict in raising me, beware of the wooden spoon, everything was for my own good. It meant she cared. She was the first woman in my life to give me a feeling of comfort and stability. We had a lot of fun together too, especially when Jack Sr. was in town. He was a jokester and always doing silly things to make us laugh. Her laughter was like music that filled up our home. It made me feel good to see Granny smile because I knew she had taken on a big responsibility to raise me. No easy task, I might add.

Summer Camp?

Granny was married to my Grandpa Tom, but he lived and worked in a small city located about 2.5 hours away. The town was Port Hope, in the tip of Michigan's thumb, but I just called it up north. My grandparents talked regularly, and they were always kind and cordial to each other. The distance helped their marriage last for over 60 years. There were a few summers when Granny packed up my stuff and took me to live with my grandpa for a month. On the first drive up north in Granny's blue

Chevy, I thought to myself, Is this her idea of summer camp? I guess she just needed a break from raising such a rambunctious young boy. After seven years of bouncing around, her willingness to send me away kind of stung. I would've rather stayed home with her.

While Grandpa Tom tried to make me feel welcome, he was no more prepared to watch after me than I was prepared for life on a farm with a man I barely knew. We didn't talk much. Grandpa was what you might call a man of few words. From what I could tell, he was stubborn and set in his ways. Sometimes, I felt like I was in his way.

Grandpa lived in an old farmhouse. He woke up every morning at 4:00 a.m. He would turn on the staticky AM radio, make his coffee, and then, steamy cup-in-hand, walk outside through his garden. I silently trailed behind him, keeping a bit of distance, watching as he squashed tomato bugs off the plants. He would say, "Jack, did you squash that one?" I remember the sun beating down on the back of my neck as the dust swirled around me on the farm. The same drill, day in and day out. It felt like torture.

There were times when I felt homesick, so I would sneak in the house and use the old, black rotary dial telephone that was attached to the kitchen wall to call Granny. I would beg her to come get me. I missed the conversation, laughter, comfort, and routine of being at home with her. I missed my friends and goofing around with them. She would tell me over the phone that it was good for me to have time with my grandpa. He did teach me the manly things that I needed to learn, like how to mow the grass, drive his stick-shift pickup truck, shoot a gun, and even squish bugs with my fingers. I realize now that Grandpa Tom also taught me the value of hard work, routine, and discipline. The day Granny picked me up from the farmhouse and took me home with her was the best day of the summer.

Home Sweet Home

As hard as the summer's away were, they helped me mature, and Granny recognized it. She gave me a sense of independence, starting in 7th grade, when we set up my bedroom in the basement. I invited my friends over to our house. We were always hungry and would stand around the kitchen, talking, laughing, and cleaning out her cupboards. She never complained. We also stayed up late, so sometimes my friends crashed at our house for the night. Granny was good with that too. When she went to bed, she would just remind us to turn off the lights. Her trust meant a lot.

We didn't have mobile phones when I was a kid, so when my friends wanted to get a hold of me, they had to call our house phone. If I wasn't home, Granny answered. She said the same thing to everyone, every time, "No, Jack's not here. Good enough." and then she hung up. To this day, without fail, she still says, "Alright, good enough" at the end of every phone conversation. I smile, knowing that's her special way of never saying goodbye. Always good enough until the next time.

The special bond that formed over time between Granny and me had cemented itself to my core, so much so that I found it hard to leave our home. I got the feeling she never wanted me to leave either. I smile, remembering how she gave me a rough time about it when I finally did move out. I was 21 and leaving the place that was my real home, and the one woman who truly loved me.

It wasn't until I was in my late 30's that I came to realize how much of a guiding light Granny had been for me. There were countless times she would look me right in the eye and say, "Jack, be happy and remember that everything else is just details." I don't think I knew what she meant when I was young, but her words of wisdom have stayed with me to this day. I now strive to live and lead in the same way.

My grandmother is now 94 years old and still sharp as a tack. Recently, I asked her to tell me more about raising me and what I was like as a young boy. Her response was classic for her generation, "You know Jack, we don't talk about personal things like that." It was like hearing the needle slide off a '78 vinyl record when she said that. It stopped me in my tracks, reminding me of the silent treatment she gave me as a young boy. I smiled and fondly looked at her across the dinner table that night. My heart was content. I sat there thinking about all of my memories that we shared over the years. I know I must have been a handful to raise, but Granny did it with a joyful heart.

I am forever grateful that Granny took me in and raised me like her own son. She provided stability and security that I needed as a child. She made me feel loved. I am certain she changed the direction of my life and helped mold me into the man I am today. I know the most important value that my granny taught me is to have a grateful mindset.

Grateful is Our Mindset.

"Your mindset can be the most significant attribute when approaching any situation. When dealing with a problem or seeing an opportunity, do your best to remember how fortunate you are to have the life you live. You can have a positive impact that can change a life and, ultimately, the world."

CHAPTER 2
Make it Right

"Never let the fire in your heart go out. Keep it alive. Serve the Lord. When you hope, be joyful. When you suffer, be patient. When you pray, be faithful. Share with God's people who are in need. Welcome others into your homes." (Romans 12:11-13 NIRV)

<u>RIGHT.</u> I am not talking about being right, but doing right.

When I was two years old, I met a man named Dave Armstrong. This amazing man has been a caring, loving father figure, and a supportive role model since the day I met him. As a kid, I thought his last name suited him well because I heard it as two words: Arm - Strong. I giggled every time I heard someone say it: Dave ARM STRONG. His arms were physically strong, but more importantly, his real strength was in his character, integrity, and loyalty. When we were together, it was comfortable and fun. I could easily see that he enjoyed life. He had a way about him that always made me feel special. When we sat and talked, it was as if I was the most important person in the world. He would often hug me and say, "Jacky, follow your dreams." Dave quickly became someone who I knew I could count on to be there for me.

Build a fireplace. Raise a son.

Dave met my mom when they were both working at Ford. When Mom and Dave were dating, I remember being so excited that I would yell out "Daddy Dave" down the aisles of the grocery store. I wanted everyone to hear it. What I didn't know back then was that Dave told my mom that hearing me say that made him feel so loved that he could never leave me. They married the year after they met. I was the happiest kid around! Dave even traded in his beloved Corvette for a 4-door Ford Mercury to make room for me. I can't label Dave as my "step-dad," so I won't, it's just not big enough. Two years after they married, my mom gave birth to my baby sister, Susan. With the four of us living together, this was my first chance to be part of a real family.

Dave was my idol; he worked hard to support my mother and our new family. In addition to working at Ford, he took on side jobs like landscaping and carpentry. In my eyes, Dave was good at everything he did. He would teach me as much as he could about all he knew. He even helped to build our home. My favorite part was the fireplace. It was the biggest, most amazing one I had ever seen. Dave was always going out of his way to do things to make me feel special. On my 5th birthday, he bought me my first bike and taught me how to ride. Another time, he had me put my footprint in the freshly-poured concrete driveway to leave my mark permanently. That simple act of love left a permanent imprint on my life.

Unfortunately, only two years after Susan was born, my mom and Dave got divorced. I was six years old at the time, and all I knew was that it felt... BAD. The day Dave told me that he and my mom were getting a divorce, I remember looking at him holding back the tears in my eyes and saying, "No, Dad, I don't want to move! We have the best fireplace on the block." To move again was tough. To have to leave Dave and the house he built for us felt like a punch in the stomach. I will never forget the sick feeling I had the day Mom drove my sister and me away.

The Strong in Armstrong

Luckily, week after week, year after year, Dave came to pick up my sister for regular parenting time. The best part was that he picked me up too, every time! You know, the strong in Armstrong? That's what I am talking about! Dave chose to be my dad. He didn't do what was easy; he did what was right. He was the first man in my life who gave me a sense of stability and belonging.

Dave and Me

After I moved in with Granny, Dave graciously told me that his door was always open, and I was welcome to live with him if I ever wanted to. He was respectful of the fact that I was living with my grandmother and Jack Sr., but his open-door invite meant a lot to me. He continued to pick me up some weekends and on special occasions like my birthday and holidays. In the winter, he would take me snowmobiling. For my 8th birthday, he built a go-kart for me. My eyes got so big when I saw it! It was awesome. I used to drive circles around his house and made a figure 8 with it in the backyard. Once in a while, he even let me take it out into the street to test its speed. When I turned 14, he put me to work by giving me a summer job with his landscaping company. I worked many long, hot days as part of his crew. It was a back-breaking, dirty job, but I enjoyed making some of my own spending money. Oh yeah, luckily I never crashed the go-kart, so he let me drive his work truck when I got my driver's license.

Since that first day God brought Dave into my life, he has always been there for me. He's my guardian angel. Forty-five years later, I know he has been my go-to-guy, my steady rock, and committed to loving my family and me. To this day, I can count on him, week after week, year after year.

He has taught me many things over the years about landscaping and carpentry. More importantly, he taught me that life is about making choices and to be fully committed to walking tall by making the tough choices, not the easy ones. I know with certainty that Dave's examples of unwavering commitment, along with his steadfast actions, have been a playbook showing me how to be a better man, a better husband, and a better father to my own four boys.

When I was growing up, Dave would sit me down and tell me, "You know Jacky, it's always on us to go the extra mile." I have carried his words of wisdom with me throughout my life. Now Dave says to me, "I didn't know you would go around the world with that mile." Even now, as I reflect on his words of wisdom to follow my dreams and go the extra mile, it makes me realize that he gave me the courage to define my journey. What a gift!

I am blessed to call Dave, my dad. I know the most important value that Dave has taught me is that you don't just do what is easy, you do what is right.

We Don't Just Do What is Easy, We Do What is Right.

Make it

"Doing what is right is not always easy. Though challenging at times, you must speak the truth and provide the best. Cultivating a mindset to do the right thing, even when it's not the easiest thing, is always the right thing to do."

Right

CHAPTER 3
Unconditional Love

Love. You know that feeling that cannot be described with words, but you can feel it deep in your heart, soul, and mind?

That's exactly how I felt the night I met Jennifer Brysse.

"*Do everything in love.*"

(1 Corinthians 16:14 NIV)

Love. **You know that feeling that cannot be described with words, but you can feel it deep in your heart, soul, and mind? That's exactly how I felt the night I met Jennifer Brysse.**

It was November 9, 1997, and my best friend Craig called me and said, "Let's go to the Red Wings game tonight. Meet me at my mom's house, and don't be late." I laughed and said, "Me late? I'm never late." A little while later, he called me again, and this time said, "You're really going to show up, right?" I thought, what's he got up his sleeve? I replied, "Dude, I'll be there!" When I hung up the phone, I had no clue how that Sunday night would change my life forever.

Craig and I grew up a few blocks from each other in the same neighborhood. I had been to his parent's house hundreds of times, but this time was different. When I pulled up in front of the house, a beautiful brunette walked out the front door.

"Hi, I'm Jenny."

"Great, I'm Jack."

At first, I didn't think much about it because Craig is from a family of six kids, so I just assumed Jenny was one of his sister's friends. Craig looked at me and grinned that same grin he gave me the first time we met in middle school. It was like he knew something I didn't.

What Craig didn't tell me was that his girlfriend Nicole and her best friend Jenny were the ones who got the hockey tickets and we were going with them. I put my hand on his shoulder, leaned in and said, "Seriously, a blind date? You know I am not looking for a girlfriend." At 25, I was having fun running the streets with my friends and traveling.

The Game Changer

It turned out that Craig did know something I didn't. Jenny and I immediately clicked. We talked non-stop on the way to Joe Louis Arena. Before we got out of the car, she grinned and told me that she liked my teeth, which made me smile even bigger. It was the best double-date: fun, relaxed, and comfortable. Score! The Wings won 6-3 over the Calgary Flames. After the victory, Craig drove us back to his house, where Jenny and I sat in my Mustang, talking until 3:00 am.

1995 Ford Mustang

It's true what they say: When you aren't looking for love is when it happens. I asked Jenny out for the next night and the night after that. We were spending all of our free time together on dinner dates and talking for hours. Jenny was everything and more than I could have ever dreamed of. She was energetic, smart, and had a great personality. After dating for three months, I asked her to go to Florida. I loved traveling and wanted to take her someplace fun. Disney World would be the perfect place to get away in February, and avoid the Michigan snow. We had a blast! Even waiting in the long lines seemed shorter. I bought matching Mickey Mouse sweatshirts that we wore everywhere. It was easy to have a great time with Jenny, and she laughed at all my jokes. Bonus! I could feel a strong connection building between us, and I was falling in love.

Even though it seemed fast (and crazy), it felt so right! Only nine months after we met, on August 9, 1998, I proposed. I had made dinner reservations at Tom's Oyster Bar in Grosse Pointe. It had been a busy day, and I wanted to first stop by Jenny's parent's house to ask for their daughter's hand in marriage. Thankfully they gave me their blessings, and I was on my way. With the stop at her parents and rush hour traffic, I was late getting to the restaurant, which caused me extra stress.

Jenny was sitting there patiently waiting for me. She looked beautiful. Words can't describe how I felt just seeing her there. I sat down and made some small talk, and I ordered a Miller Lite, then another. I was visibly sweating. Jenny looked at me, puzzled,

> "Jack, you aren't normally late for our dates, and you seem so antsy. What's going on?"

She was right; I was extremely nervous. My mind was racing. What if she said no? I would have been devastated because I was crazy about her, and I knew I didn't want to live another day without her by my side.

Mr. & Mrs.

She said YES! On August 27, 1999, less than two years from our first date, Jenny and I were married. I am so grateful to call this incredible, loving woman, my wife. Our wedding day was perfect. I had never felt happier and more at peace. With Craig and Nicole by our sides during the ceremony, it made me realize just how blessed I was that they had introduced us. Two weeks later, we returned the favor and stood up for them. It was a whirlwind — two weddings in two weeks filled with family, friends, and so many amazing memories. It's funny, Craig and I met when we were kids, as did Jenny and Nicole, yet I never met Jenny in school. The perfect person for me was right there, the whole time, in East Detroit. I guess we needed to meet at the right time, or she might not have said yes.

" To everything there is a
season, A time for every
purpose under heaven."

(Ecclesiastes 3:1 NKJV)

I sold my bachelor pad condo, and we bought our first house in Chesterfield, Michigan. Jenny was a hairstylist working out of the small salon we set up in our basement. I was working the day shift at Ford. Our married life together was humming along nicely. We started saving money and planning for our future. Both of us knew we wanted a big family. I liked the idea of our home filled with kids and noise. In God's perfect time, Jenny gave birth to four healthy boys. They are my pride and joy! I can't imagine my life without them. Nicholas was born in 2002, Andrew in 2005, Reid in 2010, and Drake in 2012. We decided to stand pat with four of a kind. We didn't want to gamble that number five wouldn't be a girl. The boys say that their mom is the backbone of the family, and I am the dreamer. Jenny and I seem to balance each other out perfectly. While I am the visionary, she is the practical one. She lets me soar like an eagle, but is also great at setting realistic boundaries with things like our finances. The boys are right. We are a perfect match, and our family wouldn't survive a day without her.

Jenny is the calming voice of reason when I take on too much. When I was a kid playing basketball, the most exciting part of the game was the first jump ball. The ref tosses the ball up, and a player from each team explodes upward to reach it and knock it to his teammate. At that moment, its "game on!" Every time I get a new idea in my head, I feel that same explosion of energy. I want to grab the ball and sprint down the court to get it started. Jenny never saw me play in school, but she knows me so well. It's like her beautiful brown eyes are piercing through me to see my mind spinning out of control.

My stress level goes way up, and she says it's obvious that I'm moving too quickly. I am a stress-eater and stress-sleeper.

Every time this happens, which Jenny says is too often, she's my never-ending coach, calmly giving me the signal to slow down the play. When I ask her to remind me not to do that again, she laughs at me, knowing it's just my nature. A great player is nothing without a great coach. I'm glad she will be there to remind me a thousand times more.

Jenny has this beautiful way about her that I can let my guard down and just be myself. It's an incredible feeling to know that she accepts me as I am and always has my back. I am a very lucky man for the level of commitment that she has shown to me, our marriage, and our family. She has two feet on solid ground but is a vital catalyst in helping to make my dreams come true.

We make sure we don't sacrifice our relationship for success. Life can be crazy. With the hectic schedule of raising four boys and the demands of work, there are times that it seems our days blur into the next. To slow things down and reconnect, we have weekly date nights at the same restaurant. We order the same bottle of wine, the same appetizer, and the same food every time. We are regulars at our favorite restaurant, and I am on a first-name basis at the flower shop. I buy Jenny flowers every week as a way of expressing my gratitude for all she does for our family and me. Her favorite color is red, and her favorite flowers are roses, which makes it easy. I guess these are examples of how I like comfort, routine, and stability in my personal life.

We talk in the morning before the boys wake up. Jenny makes me coffee, and I sit in my favorite chair by the fireplace (I do like a good fireplace). It's a quiet time in the morning just for us. We have our familiar routines like eating breakfast with the boys, driving them to school, and then heading to the gym for a workout class together. Did I mention she's a fantastic cook? Her homemade beef stroganoff, mac and cheese, and secret sauce spaghetti are some of our favorites. She makes sure we never go hungry. Our close friends say we still act like we are dating, and our son Drew even covers his eyes when he sees us kiss.

Family Vows

Keeping a healthy marriage while raising a family and building a global business has its fair share of ups and downs. To break away, in 2017, we took a family vacation to Cancun, and I planned a surprise ceremony on the beach on New Year's Eve. I wanted to renew our wedding vows in front of our sons. I felt it was important for them to see our love, loyalty, and commitment to each other. That night was memorable in every way, especially the moment when the boys thought we had gotten a divorce and then remarried. During the wedding ceremony, I took Jenny's hands, looked into her eyes, and reminded her of how grateful I was for her unconditional love. I also told her and the boys I felt blessed beyond measure by our family's love and time together. And that night on the beach with the biggest smile on my face, I shouted,

> "Fallon family: We don't throw in the towel. We will always stick together to make it work!"

For over 20 years now, Jenny has been my strength, my best friend, and my confidant. Since we met, she has been my true north staying with me through the good times and our fair share of challenges. We learn from the tough times and get through them by focusing on the good things in our lives.

When I close my eyes at night with Jenny by my side, I can still see Craig's mom pulling back the curtains in the living room looking out at us, wondering what we were doing parked in front of her house at three in the morning. The night we met, my life changed forever. We still reminisce about our first date, and Jenny kept the Red Wings ticket in her wallet for 10 years. I know the most important value that Jenny has taught me is that we love each other. Period.

We Love Each Other. Period.

Uncondit

"As humans, we are a big family. Families love each other and support each other in good times and bad. No matter what situation you face, approach it with love, and you'll never regret what you get in return."

CHAPTER 4
Always Hungry

Hungry? I love to eat food, but that's not the hungry I'm talking about.

"If you can't fly then run, if you can't run then walk, if you can't walk then crawl, but whatever you do you have to keep moving forward."

- Martin Luther King, Jr.

<u>Hungry?</u> I love to eat food, but that's not the hungry I'm talking about.

I graduated from East Detroit High School in 1991. I knew going to college just wasn't for me. I was young and content living in my Granny's basement, working odd jobs to get by.

Working for a Living

My first job of significance was cold calling for the Michigan Professional Police Association. It was a desk job, Monday through Friday, from 8 to 5. Every day was the same. I sat in a crowded room, making outbound calls from a list of random phone numbers to solicit donations from people living in Metro Detroit. Talking to so many different people made the grind a little more interesting; the more I talked, the more money they donated. The donations helped fund the training of local police officers, and I liked that my job helped people.

After a short time of working the phones, my boss promoted me to manager. He told me that I demonstrated leadership skills, and he had noticed how social I was with everyone in the office. I remember laughing out loud when he said I had the gift of gab. I was still young and pumped to get the promotion with a small raise. However, my next job opportunity was even better.

When I turned 21 years old, I thought I had hit the jackpot. I landed my dream job at Ford Motor Company, or as some people fondly call it, "Ford's." I was sure Granny was proud of me for getting a good-paying, steady job at such a well-respected automotive company.

Yes, I was one of the lucky ones who would make a good living, have unbelievable benefits, and retire after working on an assembly line for a mere 30 years. I was following in the footsteps of my mom, Dave, and even Dave's siblings. It was like a family tradition, and I was proud to be carrying the torch. Back then, nepotism was big at Ford, so I used my family connections to help get the job. It was Dave's mom, Grandma Jean, who helped me get in. I started at the Chesterfield plant on August 8, 1994. Many of my high school friends also had relatives working at Ford and were hired around the same time.

My first job on the assembly line was assisting in making car seats. Working side-by-side with my friends made it feel like we were back in high school. We worked hard on the line but made sure to have fun while we were doing it. A small group of us would drag race in the parking lot on our lunch breaks, and the laughter seemed as loud as the sound of the cars. Our daily work was based on making 500 seats for the Escort. The best part of the job was when we got our work done early. We went home and still got paid for the remainder of our shift. I liked the luxury of working with my friends and getting paid to leave early. A dream come true, right?

I made some new friends, one was John Licari.

We met in 1994 and quickly became close buds. John was an honest man with a strong work ethic. I could sense the love he had for his family and was drawn to his big heart. Little did I know that this friendship I valued in my 20's would last a lifetime. We hung out after work on weekdays and went to family parties on the weekends. As the years passed, we even attended each other's weddings. We stuck together through thick and thin within our own self-created "Ford fraternity." It truly felt like a second family.

I was all in as a Ford man. In my first three years of working there, I bought a new Ford Ranger, a Thunderbird, and a Mustang. Yes, the same black convertible Mustang that Jenny and I ended up sitting in until 3:00 am talking on the night we met.

Oh, and about my beloved Mustang. Another one of my new friends at work was a guy named Nino. He asked to borrow my 'Stang for a date on a Friday night; he wanted to impress a girl. His old work truck was not impressive. Of course he could borrow my car; that's what friends do. That night after their date, Nino was driving home, testing out the horsepower of the V8 engine, when he had a second date with a tree. It was a fast car! He totaled my Mustang. He called me and said, "I wrecked your car, but Jack, the date was love at first sight!" I didn't even get mad at him because, in the back of my mind, I knew exactly how Nino felt; it was the same way I had felt the night I met Jenny. It's the car crash story with a happy ending. Nino and his date were married a few years later, and Jenny and I attended their wedding.

Monotony Takes Its Toll

As the years went by, employees and friends were moved from one Ford factory to another, and the job began to grow tiresome for me. It felt like there was no relief in sight until retirement, which was still almost 20 years away. By June of 2005, I was working in the Utica plant, where the line went very slowly. Now I was making dashboards, and there was no leaving work early when we finished our quota for the day. We would sit around bored, waiting to clock out. The fun had faded.

I would see long-time workers hobble into the factory slowly, work even slower, and then miraculously run for the door at the end of the day. It wasn't uncommon for some employees to drink their lunch — regardless of the time of day. The liquid lunch was accompanied by smoking and, of course, the constant complaining as they counted the years they had left until retirement. Some of the guys called it their life sentence.

I had some positive routines in my life, but this was one place where routine didn't work for me. Working on the line in a factory was very repetitive. Doing the same process day after day made my mind go numb. It felt like a "benefit handcuff." What I mean is, the great pay and benefits kept me cuffed to a job that didn't fill me up or allow me to grow and pursue my dreams. I kept asking myself, is this really my script for life? Every night, I would sit quietly, pray, and ask God for guidance.

Time passed, and I found myself dreading going to work each day. Jenny nearly pushed me out the door every morning. I felt like a robot doing mindless work. At the end of my shift, I would go home feeling discouraged. I would complain to Jenny, "There has to be something different for me to do in life." While the factory job was great for some, it just didn't feel right for me. I was always hungry to learn more, do more, and make more of myself. I was sure I wanted more for my career and my family. I decided it was time for me to pursue new challenges. I was determined to break free from the benefit handcuff so I could rewrite the old family legacy and create a new one for myself.

"Show me your ways, LORD,
teach me your paths."

(Psalm 25:4 NIV)

Rewriting the Family Legacy

Just like Dave, many of my hardworking co-workers took on side jobs in landscaping and carpentry. I admired them, but I didn't want a side job. I wanted and needed something that would challenge me mentally and could grow into something permanent. I began to see success all around me with network marketing companies, and I was intrigued. In 1997, I started working part-time as a sales representative for ACN, a reseller of long-distance telephone services. It was fascinating to see how the business operated. I was given opportunities to learn that made me think in new ways that working in the factory didn't require or allow. The part of my brain that had only been along for the ride was kicking into gear.

I would work at Ford during the day and research the ins and outs of network marketing at night. I was fortunate to have two incredible mentors, the twin brothers who helped found ACN, Mike and Tony Cupisz. They generously took me under their wings and taught me everything they knew about multi-level marketing. I was feeding the appetite that I hadn't even known was there. I felt mental growth for the first time in my life. While Mike and Tony were only a few years older than me, they were already extremely successful in the business and inspirational leaders. They had a unique ability to connect with people and make them feel special. Who doesn't want to feel special?

It was time for my first sale. Of course, it had to be to my best friends, so I signed up Craig and John for the phone service without telling them. I was saving them money, after all; that's what friends do. I even recruited my close friend Scott to work part-time with me at ACN. He was a full-time teacher. He picked the business up fast and talked a lot about it, but this side gig only lasted about six months for him. He flat-out told me that being in sales just wasn't in his blood. I wasn't sure what was in my blood, but whatever it was, it was running fast through my veins. It was mentally intoxicating!

Mike and Tony always went out of their way to help me learn and grow with a new business mindset. They pushed me like never before, teaching me about personal and professional development, as well as the importance of having the right attitude. They would pile books on me to read. My favorite was *Think and Grow Rich* by Napoleon Hill. This book is the granddaddy of all self-help books. I stayed up late reading to satisfy my newfound hunger for knowledge.

There were nights when dinners with Mike and Tony would last four or five hours just talking about setting goals and achieving them. I soaked up every minute of it. I was grateful to have these two mentors invest so much of their time and energy in me. I worked part-time for ACN for four years. It gave me the wake-up call I needed, and I came out with the knowledge to take on the industry myself.

First Headquarters

Big Changes

In 1999, I felt ready to go solo and start my own little company. I thought, why not?

I still had my full-time job at Ford, and I was stoked to become an entrepreneur. I set up shop in our basement alongside Jenny's hair salon. My day shift couldn't end fast enough for me to get home, where I worked night after night to set up my own multi-level marketing business. Starting anything new can seem overwhelming, but I knew there was no room in my mind for doubt. I just kept telling myself to be resilient while also hearing Daddy Dave's advice in my head telling me to follow my dreams.

In 2008, Ford offered buyout programs to some of its employees. I had worked there for 14 years, so my net buyout was $50,000. Believe me, at age 36, it was all-consuming to think about walking away from my seniority, good pay, and generous benefits. The stress and uncertainty of the unknown of running my own business full time felt overwhelming. It certainly would take perseverance and tenacity to be a successful entrepreneur.

The weight of the decision felt like an elephant sitting on my chest. There were days I could hardly breathe, and my head was spinning. I told myself, this is a once-in-a-lifetime chance to get paid a lump sum of money to leave a job and push yourself into a new career. Jenny and I discussed the pros and cons:

"I have to be all in 100% to make it work!"

"Jack, we have two young boys, and it is a scary time for us to give up the security of your job at Ford."

She spoke calmly, but her concerns were clear, and I knew she was right. It was a risky financial decision because although my buyout was a decent amount, it wasn't enough to keep my business afloat for very long. Our conversation continued around the clock for days about whether I should stay at Ford. We knew that it was a giant leap of faith.

Together, Jenny and I decided to take the buyout.

You know how the first time you ride a roller coaster, you're not sure if you want to hold on tightly or let go and reach your arms up into the air? That was my final day at the factory. Ironically, I remember crying as I walked out of the Ford plant for the last time. After more than a decade of working on the factory line, I was letting go and leaving comfort and stability — two things that gave me a sense of security. I wiped away my tears as I opened my car door, thinking about the good memories with the people who had become my close friends. When I pulled out of the parking lot, I felt a sudden thrilling rush of freedom. It was like a wave of peace came over me. Right then, my mind replayed a line from one of my favorite movies, *The Shawshank Redemption*, "Get busy living or get busy dying." I smiled all the way home. I couldn't wait to hug Jenny and the boys and get busy living.

What I realized through this significant career change was that I had to believe in myself and take risks that put me outside of my comfort zone. When I opened my mind to new possibilities, I found the famous quote by Alexander Graham Bell to ring true, "When one door closes, another one opens."

I am incredibly grateful for the encouragement and leadership of my business mentors, Mike and Tony Cupisz. They recognized my untapped potential and pushed me to learn and grow as a businessman. I know the most important value that Mike and Tony taught me is to always be hungry for more.

We Are Always Hungry For More.

Hungry

"To stay hungry for more, you must find a way to stay ahead of the curve. If you cultivate a life that thrives on this concept, it will keep you from being complacent or satisfied with the norm. Continually reinvent yourself, look for a better way to do things, and you'll always be hungry."

for More

CHAPTER 5
Be Passionate

*" People buy into the leader
before they buy into the vision."*

- John C. Maxwell

Passion. Do you remember a time you felt truly passionate about something? I found my passion in my basement.

Walking away from my job at Ford in 2008 was a major decision. Jenny and I knew that there was no way I would've been satisfied working in the factory for the rest of my life. It was time to turn my dreams into reality. I couldn't turn the volume down on the voice in my head. It was like hearing the unmistakable sound of Morgan Freeman saying to me, "Challenge yourself; it's the only path which leads to growth." I realized it was my subconscious telling me it was time to do more with my life. After taking the buyout, I was able to dedicate all my time to something I was more passionate about. I felt empowered and ready to take on the world.

A New Kind of Hunger

I want to begin by taking you back, before the buyout, to those days in 1999 when I started my own network marketing business in the basement of our house. My days began with the early shift at Ford from 6:00 am to 2:00 pm, and couldn't end fast enough. I would race home and run down the basement steps where I worked until at least 10:00 pm. Most nights, Jenny would bring dinner downstairs and keep me company while I talked more than I ate. Jenny sat patiently and listened to all of my thoughts and dreams come spilling out.

While I had never been much of a reader in school, I was now hungry for new knowledge. I became a voracious reader of personal and professional self-help books. I would get pumped up listening to books on tape in my truck. When I was assembling dashboards, my mind was wandering about different products that I wanted to sell, and what I thought would sell. My research showed that people all over the world spent millions of dollars each year buying products to make themselves feel better, lose weight, and lead a healthier lifestyle. That's how I knew I wanted to focus on the health and wellness industry.

The First Product

My goal was to develop a product that made you feel better when you took it, something good for you, and of course, it had to taste good. From my own experience, who cares how good something is for you if you can't stand the taste? I worked non-stop for two years with a small manufacturing company in the U.S. to develop our first product, which was a liquid multi-vitamin. It took several versions to get it just right for nutritional value, color, and taste. NutraBurst® was born. I came up with the name to represent the burst of nutrition in each serving.

I had all of my time and our money wrapped up in this one product. It was a critical juncture in our start-up business that could go only one of two ways: a successful new product that people bought, loved, and bought again or total failure. It was the moment of truth. Could I turn my passion into a business that could make a difference in people's lives?

Time for Change

I am often asked how I came up with the company name. First and foremost, my goal was to convey change. I wanted to be a caring company by helping people change their lives. I wanted to show people that I cared about their health and well-being, personal development, as well as to feel a sense of family and a spiritual connection.

Late one night, I sat alone in the rare quiet of the basement, thinking of what I wanted to name my company. I thought,

Change.

Change their lives.

Totally change their lives.

Total changes.

Total Life Changes.

Finally, it became crystal clear in my mind. The name was perfect! Total Life Changes (TLC) was officially launched in 2003. I quickly filed the LLC company name papers and paid $100 to an online graphic design company to come up with the first logo. This was an important step to be able to develop the packaging for NurtraBurst® and create related sales and marketing materials.

Johnny be Good

John Licari and I had become close friends while working together at Ford. He knew that I was very interested in starting my own business. While John wasn't as enthusiastic about the idea as I was, he saw my passion and agreed to work with me a few hours each evening. There were times he even took overflow calls at his house late at night.

We didn't want to seem like a small company, so we would use different names to make it appear that more than two guys were taking calls. In the spirit of having fun, when we answered the phone, we would use names from the famous 1960's music group, the Jersey Boys. The funniest part was when a customer would call back and ask to speak to Frankie, Tommy, Nick, or Vinnie. We would look at each other and crack up laughing because we couldn't remember who had taken the call and which name we had used. When a sale was made, we rang a large bell to celebrate our success. The sound fueled us to keep the momentum going, take the next call, and make the next sale.

For the record, the rumor is true. I do love country music. But in the basement, I played the Backstreet Boys CD over and over. I sang every word to every song until Johnny would beg me to turn it off. I kept singing the lyrics to "As Long As You Love Me" as loudly as I could to partly annoy him and let him know we were in this for the long haul. We laughed a lot, and day-by-day our friendship grew stronger.

We were a strong team. I could feel the synergy, but I could also tell that John didn't love working late every night. His heart just wasn't in it. He was there as a loyal friend and to make a little extra cash. It was clear to me that John's career potential was much bigger than he was aware of. I needed to find a way for him to believe in himself and in me. I hoped to win him over eventually and get him to work full time. John could be so much more than an accessory to my vision. My goal was to have him play a vital role in the success of my company.

Within 18 months, my vision became clear to him; we were both hooked on helping people! Our passion for making a positive impact on people's lives became real. I had found my purpose! There were days that we felt like we were on top of the world. Total Life Changes (TLC) was becoming a company that both our sales representatives and customers referred to as tender loving care. It was rewarding to realize I had accomplished my dream of creating and building a caring company.

Many years later, Johnny told me that if I had been able to articulate my vision early on, he would have wholeheartedly bought in much sooner. He has always enjoyed helping people, but it wasn't until he saw that we were helping thousands that it finally sunk in. I guess he had to figure it out for himself. John apologized to me for not buying in earlier. Of course, no apology was necessary from my close friend. I was so glad he finally saw my vision. It all made sense to me when Johnny said, "Jack, when the heart buys in, it happens." We both believe the timing was God's plan.

The First Roadblock

Running my own company felt exhilarating, like racing down an empty freeway in my dream car, a 1969 Ford Mustang Mach 1 5.8-liter Windsor V8. But there were also times where I felt like my speed was too fast, and it reminded me of when I let Nino borrow my Mustang.

I clearly remember April 21, 2005, for two reasons. On the positive side, Jenny was in the hospital having our second son, Andrew. Welcoming our second healthy baby boy into our family was like the high of driving fast in the Mach 1. On the low side, the business had hit a concrete roadblock — a $15,000 one to be exact, which felt like I crashed and burned.

Based on my upbringing by my granny, I choose to see the good in people and give them the benefit of the doubt. I had trusted someone to help me grow my business. Unfortunately, this guy turned out to be a con man. I will call him, "Mr. Merchant Mafia." I'll spare the details. Let's just say that he was smooth and convinced me he would take my business to the moon and back. I should have known better and realized it was too good to be true. I know, as you are reading this right now, you are probably yelling at me, "Jack, what were you thinking?" After all, that's what everyone was screaming at me back then. I was beyond disappointed because I had lost a lot of money by trusting a man who lied to my face.

I had to tell Jenny that I needed to draw against our home equity line of credit (again). It would drain it to zero. We were out of money. She was holding our newborn baby, making it an even tougher conversation. With my head down, I added,

> "I know this is a set back for us, but I believe something good will come out of this situation."

I said it out loud that day to also try to convince myself. Her facial expression said everything, "This was a painful financial blow." Once again, Jenny stood faithfully by my side. Together, we agreed that we would not let this ruin us, taint our dreams, or stop us from moving forward. When I drove her and Andrew home from the hospital, I remember telling her I believed that someone always leads me to the next person I am supposed to meet. I still believe it to this day: for every person I meet in life, there is a purpose. It may not be evident at the time, but it will eventually become clear. Instead of feeling defeated, Jenny and I became smarter, stronger, and better because of it.

Help Wanted

Our basement had become our epicenter. Jenny was doing hair for her clients, and I had set up shop next to her. Jenny asked her mom, Loretta, to help babysit our boys while we both worked. Loretta would show up at 7:00 am to babysit, but soon she was answering the phone, taking orders, and shipping the packages. My mother-in-law was great with finances, so I asked her to take over keeping the books. Having Loretta's help every day gave me time to focus on growing the business with our sales representatives. I was also ready to develop a new product. By 2006, Loretta was working full time for TLC, setting up customer accounts, and the company website.

"*I can do all things through Christ who strengthens me.*"

(Philippians 4:13 NKJV)

Thirsty for More

In 2008, we launched Iaso® Tea. I worked for about six months with a U.S. manufacturer to come up with a proprietary blend, with the benefits of being an all-natural detox and cleansing tea. We were thrilled about this new TLC product.

As you can imagine, I quickly blew through the cash from my Ford buyout. The stakes were high, and so was the stress. Jenny and I refinanced our home to secure the money I needed to pay for product development, packaging, and shipping. It took a lot longer than I could have ever imagined to gain some traction in the direct sales space.

We didn't have any outside funding, angel investors, or business partners. I was 100% owner and determined to do what I could with the limited resources we had. It also meant draining our savings account if needed. It was definitely a slow and steady business approach. In my mind, I was running a fast 100-yard dash, but in reality, I was running a marathon in slow motion (like at a 30-minute mile pace). We were living hand-to-mouth for quite a while. It was several years before I ever took a real paycheck. I knew the money we had was better spent on creating the best products, providing the best commission for the sales representatives, and paying our valued employees. The sacrifice paid off.

After two years, we had more orders for NutraBurst® and Iaso® Tea than Loretta, John, and I could handle. I was excited to be gaining momentum in sales. Our days were jam-packed, and the sun never seemed to stay out long enough. Because we were in a residential area, the large deliveries couldn't be made to our house. We made daily trips to the trucking terminal, near the Detroit Airport, to pick up the shipments from Utah. Every pallet had 30 cases, and we had to carry each case down to the basement. Each day, we would prepare packages for shipping, take them back up to my truck, and drive to the local post office. It was a stair-climbing workout!

Call in the Troops

A few more months passed, and we were desperately in need of help to handle the volume of orders. I needed people I could trust, so I turned to my family. In 2010, I recruited Dave, my uncles Jim and Ron, and my mom to come to help us to answer phones, process orders, and ship packages. We had cars and people coming and going all day long. I didn't care how noisy or busy it was because I was a man on a mission. There were days when our house felt less like our home and more like a crowded, busy warehouse. I didn't know how long we would be here, but as long as we were here it would be a good time.

My family members had already retired from their full-time jobs and would show up every day to work in the basement. We were pretending to be a big company while operating on a shoestring budget. With the blow dryer running, the dog barking, and our boys playing in the background, we were making sales. My Uncle Ron said we were a ragtag group of people with no business experience, but the tenacity to figure it out and the passion for getting it done. There was only one thing I could say to that: "Amen!"

There were days when Granny would stop over to visit her great-grandsons. I loved having her in our home with the boys. She made it clear to me that she had no interest in our business. She thought for sure we were doing something crazy like selling drugs. Some days, it was hard for me to believe what we were doing. I felt like I was running a covert operation. Instead, we were positively changing thousands of lives by selling NurtraBurst and Iaso® Tea, and a lot of it.

The Second Roadblock

We were selling so much that the merchant card processing companies held back the money they owed us for an extended period. Our cash was on hold. This never happened before. We were in a jam. We couldn't make payroll and didn't have the money to pay commissions to our sales representatives. Everyone was frustrated. Our home equity line of credit was already maxed out. Thank goodness for Loretta, who graciously offered to draw $20,000 out of her personal savings account to tide us over.

Jenny was not waiving the cheerleader pom-poms for me this time. I didn't feel a lot of love in the house, especially when Jenny wanted to know when this "mess" was going to end. Ouch, that hurt! Of course, I didn't blame her for being upset because it was her mom who had to bail me out this time. Jenny had a private meeting with John. She told him this was not going the way it should. She thought we should open a car wash or start a safer business because TLC was turning out to be anything but stable. Johnny didn't tell me what he said to Jenny that day to convince her to let us continue the business. If I had to guess, his big heart and empathy made him know precisely what she needed to hear.

These roadblocks were life lessons that taught me to trust my gut instinct, follow my passion, and have my eyes wide open. I was determined to hammer it out and not give up. From my part-time job at ACN, and all of my research and planning, I knew my business model worked. Even after the financial setbacks, Jenny and John were still my biggest supporters. Fortunately, Loretta just went with the flow. She has always been a supportive mother-in-law. She trusted that I would pay her back, which I did.

Does Anyone Speak Spanish?

Network marketing is so powerful that before we knew it, our business began growing in Central America. And, of course, none of us knew a word of Spanish (unless you count, Hola, Gracias, and Margarita). We desperately needed someone fluent in Spanish to take the incoming calls for the orders.

Our neighbor, Maryann, knew a woman named Rosa, who worked at JCPenney. I begged Maryann to have Rosa talk with me. She asked her five times before Rosa agreed. She was skeptical, and with good reason. Rosa had a stable job working for a major retail store. Why would she want to talk to a stranger who was working out of his basement? At the same time, Jenny was feeling the daily pressure. She reminded me that we already had Johnny and five family members working in our home. I understood her hesitation to bring in even more people, especially strangers.

Rosa Armenta

I had to prove to everyone that my passion for changing people's lives was much bigger than me.

I sent Loretta to interview Rosa at a local Panera. I believed my mother-in-law would be the perfect person to determine if Rosa would be a good fit. I told Loretta that if she liked Rosa, then bring her back to the house. After only about 20 minutes of talking, they pulled into the driveway! It was clear to me that Rosa was the perfect person for the job. She had a positive attitude, and Spanish was her first language. I offered her a job on the spot.

That same day, I asked Rosa if she was ready to travel the world? Obviously, she had only known me for a few minutes. She looked at me like I was crazy, but said, "Yes!" I stood there and grinned, knowing this was another step in the right direction. Rosa immediately started taking calls. Our customers loved her, and she was a natural with helping people.

After a couple of months, Rosa said to me, "I know, you know where you want to be. But I can't see your vision because you're always so many steps ahead of us." Her puzzled tone made me realize something important. I had to prove to everyone that my passion for changing people's lives was much bigger than me. It went way beyond my own success to helping other people succeed in life.

Two years later, it was really happening; Rosa was traveling the world representing TLC. She had already gone to El Salvador in Central America, Columbia in South America, and Las Vegas, Nevada. During that time, I hired two additional employees who were also fluent in Spanish. They took calls alongside Rosa. These three women were fantastic at building rapport with our customers and handling any service-related issues. This was vitally important since, at that time, over 90% of the incoming calls were spoken in Spanish.

We were firing on all 8 cylinders. Every day, I woke up, fueled by passion. We were growing and expanding into other countries with sales in Mexico, the Dominican Republic, Costa Rica, and Guatemala. They were busy, but fun times filled with laughter. We had our daily routine to get the work done. I was completely satisfied and comfortable in our small space, surrounded by my friends and family.

Leaving the Basement

Although a big part of me was comfortable in the basement, I knew we couldn't keep the operation there. We were bursting at the seams with products and people nearly tripping over each other every time we turned around. It was important for me to solidify the business and prove it was a viable company with the potential to grow even larger. I needed to make it clear in the minds of my family that this was real. If they could see and believe in my vision, then eventually the world would recognize us and see it too.

There were days that customers showed up at our house to buy more products. Google Maps didn't exist back then, but they still found us. That's when it hit me, my family needed their privacy back. Also, our employees, vendors, shipments, and customers all needed a real business location to go to each day. It would be a big step to take the company to the next level. I needed to find an affordable building to rent and have a steady stream of income to pay for the property taxes, insurance, office furniture, utilities, and of course, payroll.

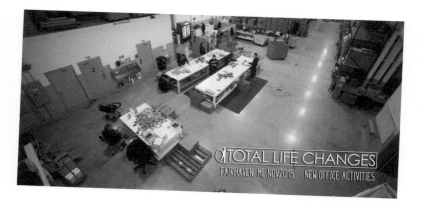

The Warehouse

In the late summer of 2011, Loretta and I looked for buildings to rent. We found an old warehouse in Ira Township, only 10 miles from our house. There was no air conditioning and only overhead infrared heat, but the location was perfect. It was jeans and a t-shirt kind of place. I signed a 5-year lease thinking this large building would comfortably house all of us for a long time.

Little did I know then, that our Iaso® Tea would grow so rapidly that in four years, we would outgrow the space. We were up to

50 employees and processing 500-600 orders per day, filling five large 40-foot shipping containers. We were out of space. I had to rent an additional end unit in the same building where we moved all of the products and shipping operations.

When we started in the basement, we had two phone lines. In the warehouse, we installed eight. Our call volume was similar to the QVC Home Shopping Network with a call every half second. It was incredible. We grew five times our sales volumes in late 2014 and into 2015. Now our headquarters has over 100 lines.

Supply and Demand

At one point, we ran out of our number one seller, Iaso® Tea. We were literally selling more than the manufacturer could produce. It will go down in TLC history as the "Great Tea Shortage of 2015."

It was nothing I could have ever anticipated. We were behind 70,000 orders with a five-week delay. When we finally restocked, it was all hands on deck without reprieve. I kept telling everyone, "Push. Push. Push!" The tea shortage caused total havoc with orders, credit card chargebacks, cash flow issues, and a social media outcry for more tea. In a word: CHAOS! We always knew people across the world loved our tea, but this was unimaginable. It felt like I was letting so many people down. I would not let it break my spirit. I knew I would find something positive out of every negative thing that was happening.

It took us three months to find two new U.S. manufacturers that could keep up with the demand. It was a business lesson in basic economics. We had to remove the product from our website so we could catch up. A few months later, we came out on the other side - exhausted, but back in the tea business. The positive outcome of this unforeseen situation was that the new manufacturers worked with us to develop and package a salable instant version of our original Iaso® Tea. The launch of a new version of our already number one selling product was a huge victory for all of us.

"Teamwork is the ability to work together toward a common vision. The ability to direct individual accomplishments toward organizational objectives. It is the fuel that allows common people to attain uncommon results."

-Andrew Carnegie

The Basement Served its Purpose

I discovered my passion in my basement. My passion runs deeply for people. My purpose is to make an impact on the world.

Looking back, we probably stayed in the basement for two years too long. It was the comfort of knowing exactly how each day would play out that kept me there. I had spent 10 years staring at those concrete walls feeling the dampness all the way to my bones. I needed the time to grow mentally and spiritually through the emotional roller coaster of good times, financial struggles, and challenging times. It reminds me of another line from the movie, *The Shawshank Redemption*, when the character Red says, "These walls are funny. First you hate 'em. Then you get use to 'em. Enough time passes, you get to depend on them...".

I depended on those basement walls for my sanctity. They served a greater purpose by helping me to focus on what was important, which was my passion. The walls gave me a place to concentrate on the good in my life, which were the blessings. I could not have done this on my own. I was blessed to have Jenny by my side every step of the way. I depended on my family and friends for their support and willingness to believe in me and my vision. What we learned from working in the basement is that we could accomplish our dreams by being passionate about changing people's lives. Passion was our fuel.

Passion is Our Fuel.

"Your passion for delivering a feeling of care and love can be the very fuel for your day. Every interaction is a new opportunity to change someone's life. If passion drives you every day, those around you will most definitely feel it."

CHAPTER 6
Have Fun

"Even though you are growing up,
you should never stop having fun."

- Nina Dobre

Fun. Who doesn't want to laugh and have fun? I sure do!

I liked school, but not exactly for all the right reasons. I felt bored in class, and I didn't like studying. No wonder Granny was always after me to do better when she saw my report card. Hindsight, right? The only reason I really wanted to go to school was for the social aspect of being with my friends. Even when I was sick, I was up on time and out the door. I would sit in the common areas of the building so I could hang out and laugh with my friends. Being sick never stopped me from having fun. It's true, laughter is the best medicine.

I remember a time when some of my friends were hanging out under the football field bleachers after school. They were trying to get me to chew tobacco. They said,

"Come on, Jack. We've all tried it. What are you waiting for?"

I thought how bad could it be, I was pretty sure my Grandpa Tom chewed. My brief hesitation was followed by them egging me on even more:

"Put a dip under your lip, Fallon."

"OK, fine! Give me some."

So, I wedged a wad of chewing tobacco between my cheek and gum, like I knew what I was doing. It got kind of juicy in my mouth, so I swallowed my spit. You can imagine what happened next. All of a sudden, my face turned green. Before I knew it, my lunch was all over the ground. My friends stood there, laughing at me and my weak stomach. I can laugh about it now, but needless to say, that was not my kind of fun!

Throughout school, I played team sports. Being part of a team appealed to me. I was on the football, basketball, and baseball teams. It wasn't because I was an All-American athlete with a dream of making it to the pros. It just felt good to be a part of something where everyone has their job, and you have to trust each other. You build that special bond and a sense of camaraderie. You are a part of a group of people working hard together to win. It's an energy that is contagious! I loved that feeling then, and I still do today.

"If it's not fun, you're not doing it right." – Bob Basso

I noticed a pattern throughout my life that when I was having fun, I naturally got more done. This was true when I played sports in school, worked on the assembly line in my 20's, and started my business in my 30's. Obviously, not everything in life is fun. I get that. We all have times in our lives that are stressful and days that seem overwhelming. Fun isn't only about constant laughter and play. When I focus on being grateful for the people and good things in my life, I have more fun. When you meet your future spouse, finish your work ahead of time, avoid a bad situation, and see your hard work pay off, it's fun! I make a conscious choice every day to have a positive attitude and find humor whenever I can. Someday's are easier than others, but that doesn't stop me.

I love team sports, teamwork, and team TLC. I want to share some stories about my TLC leadership team. These guys are three of my close friends. True friends have your back, even when you don't see things the same way. It's about trust. Some of my favorite memories are from the times I spent with them having fun and working hard to get more done.

Craig and Me

My Lifelong Friend

I met Craig Cole when I was seven years old. To me, he was just "Cole." We played little league football together for the East Detroit Tiger-Cats. We made a great team. From the moment we met, Craig and I were playing ball, telling jokes, and trying to stay out of trouble. We both went to Oakwood Middle School in Detroit and East Detroit High School. Sometimes I would hang out at his house. He had five siblings, and I liked that his house was always filled with noise.

After graduation from high school, Cole and I still hung out. I liked to make the most of my Saturdays, so I would get to his house by 8:00 in the morning. I walked in the back door, went straight to his room, and yelled, "Let's go, Cole!" When I had an adventure in mind, I always brought him along. We started the day at 8:30 and often wouldn't get home until the clock said AM again.

I didn't see Cole much when I was working in the basement. He would stop by to have Jenny cut his hair and check in on how the business was going. Craig had followed in his dad's footsteps and worked in law enforcement for 23 years. I remember the day he called to tell me he had been promoted to Sergeant. While we talked, I stopped working and looked out the window. I could hear the pride in his voice, and I felt a deep sense of admiration, knowing what he had accomplished. Craig dedicated his career to helping people by protecting their safety and security.

Fortunately, now I see him every day. As I mentioned earlier, when I've got an idea, I like to bring Cole along. I knew I wanted him on my leadership team at TLC, so in 2018, I had a heart-to-heart conversation with him. We talked on a Friday afternoon, and he started on Monday. Craig now works full-time as our Human Resources Manager/Security & Safety Lead.

In May of 2019, I took the opportunity to recognize my lifelong friend at the "You'll Feel It" TLC event in Detroit. I awarded Craig the TLC Corporate Ring for being an incredibly loyal, honest man who has supported me in every way since we met in 1979. He is the perfect wingman, and there are no limits to his friendship. We surprised him by inviting his wife, Nicole, and their two children, Ayden and Brooklyn, to the event to watch him receive his award.

Remember, Craig introduced me to Jenny. When he set me up on that blind date, I remember saying, "Oh, here we go, Cole."

That night changed my life. We have come so far together, and now it's like the circle of life is coming around again as we watch our kids grow and have fun. They even call each other cousins when we celebrate our children's birthdays together and spend the holidays as one big family. The best part is having my home filled with lots of kids and hearing all the noise like at Craig's house when we were young. We share a brotherly love that can't be replaced. We both felt that being part of a team made us better people. We may not be perfect people, but we are perfect friends. Our fun is teamwork and family.

The Guy with the Big Heart

I met John Licari in 1994 while working at the same Ford plant in Chesterfield. Since factory work was a daily grind, we had to do everything we could think of to have fun. Dumb jokes would be flying, and we were constantly poking fun at each other. Our goal was to see who could make the other laugh louder. I was always singing songs that John didn't like, just to bug him. He didn't have time to plug his ears with the car seats coming down the line. I figured if I talked non-stop, sang songs, and focused on the positive, it would make the days go by faster. John and I planned fun activities for our friends at work. Sometimes it was as simple as having everyone play cards on our breaks. People called us the life of the party, or as we were known at the plant, the life of the assembly line. Even our supervisors started to have fun with us. The morale in our area was always the highest in the factory.

John and Me

Our fun times carried over from working at the Ford plant to 2003 when I asked him to come to work part-time for me in my basement. I was serenading John with the Backstreet Boys, and he kept me laughing by making up different names from the Jersey Boys when he answered the phone. By 2006, Johnny had become my right-hand man, and I asked him to work full-time.

Our kind of fun is different. It's about connecting with people and lifting their spirits. We both enjoy life and find humor whenever possible. We laugh at ourselves all the time for doing and saying crazy stuff. John and I firmly believe that it's so much better to go through life being optimistic rather than pessimistic. Our glass is always half full.

In January 2017, John came up with the idea for TLC Fun Fridays. When he first told me about the concept, I was hesitant. I wondered if people would interrupt what they were doing to tune in to a Facebook Livestream every Friday at 2:00 p.m. Johnny convinced me that it was a great idea.

"Jack, people's attitudes are a reflection of their leadership."

"You're absolutely right. Count me in!"

What John said immediately got to me. We had a responsibility to make ourselves available in a very real way to motivate people in a non-scripted format. With John as the anchorman, Fun Fridays give us a unique opportunity to have fun and share our passion with our TLC family.

Johnny is a good man with a huge heart that he wears on his sleeve. I have believed in him since the day we met on the assembly line. John now works as the Chief Operating Officer. He is a dynamic leader and the voice of TLC. I can't imagine a day at TLC without his leadership.

Scott and me

The Teacher

I met Scott Bania in 1997. Scott and I got our hair cut at the salon where our girlfriends worked. As Jenny and Kelly's friendship blossomed, the four of us started to spend more time together. We all lived in Chesterfield, which made it easy to go on double dates. We had fun rollerblading in the fall along Metro Parkway or riding snowmobiles in the winter over a frozen creek that led us out to Lake St. Clair.

Scott's family owned a cabin about a 4.5-hour drive north from where we lived. We had a group of 10 guys that would go to the cabin for a weekend every fall. There was a sense of freedom riding 4-wheelers along the wooded trails. Our chant was, "Us boys like our toys!" There's nothing better than riding a quad through the woods with the throttle wide open. We would stop at a clearing and turn off the machines. After sitting there for at least an hour enjoying nature, the silence felt like a week back home. The comfort of quiet in the woods is a peaceful thing, especially when sitting next to your close friends.

During our weekends at the cabin, some of us would go into town for dinner and grab a few beers. One night, some hometown boys didn't like us crowding the bar. They asked what we were doing in their bar. We told them that we didn't want any trouble, but they didn't seem to buy it. I could tell things were about to go sideways. I turned to Scott and said under my breath, "I'm not looking for a fight. I'm going to get the truck. Meet me out back." Like an episode of *The Dukes of Hazzard*, Scott threw some money on the bar and ran out the back door. He jumped in my truck, and

I peeled out of there with gravel flying up, leaving a trail of dust behind us. That's one of those stories that never gets old. Our kind of fun is camaraderie and sticking together to avoid a bar fight.

After college, Scott dedicated his career to public education. For nearly 20 years, he was a Detroit Public School teacher. In 2012, I asked him to join my team. He looked at me and said, "Don't tell me it's a sales job!" We laughed about his short-lived sales gig with me many years ago. He agreed to work part-time at TLC. He worked both jobs for four years until I finally got to him. That's when I offered him a full-time job. Scott is now the Chief Communications Officer. It's fantastic having him on the TLC leadership team because he is always teaching me new things, like his favorite quote by John C. Maxwell. "People do not care how much you know until they know how much you care." It's the perfect quote since TLC is a caring company.

Never Stop Having Fun

Think about it, when we were young, everything we did was based around having fun. We were encouraged to play, laugh, and be curious as a way to learn and make friends. Did you ever notice that there is a youthful innocence when we can laugh at ourselves? Laughter takes away stress or worry and makes us think more clearly. I feel more optimistic when I incorporate fun into my daily routine. I am motivated to do more. It's simple. Humor makes life more enjoyable. I know that having fun has helped me get through some tough times in life and keep a positive attitude.

Work Hard. Play Hard.

In 2016, we were in New Orleans for the TLC Awards. I wanted to make this event epic. We were literally rolling out the red carpet and hosting a formal masquerade ball at the Hyatt Regency. With 2,000 VIP tickets sold, this was one of the largest events in the company's history. It was also the event that had the most challenges.

Never give up

We made sure to keep our spirits up with jokes and sarcasm.

Since this event was bigger than anything we had ever done, we hired an event planner. She was in charge of hiring guest speakers, scheduling the entertainment, and overseeing the jam-packed weekend of activities. Thursday night was our leadership prep meeting. That's when we found out from the event planner that she had nothing planned for Friday, our kick-off day. She had product commercials, and Michael Jackson and Prince impersonators lined up for Saturday, but nothing for Friday. Not a single thing! I couldn't believe what I was hearing. Fortunately, John and Scott were by my side, and they assured me they were committed to working all night to figure it out. We stayed up until 4 a.m. pulling things together and developing the run of the show. Thank goodness we had the support of a former designer and a bunch of TLC employees on-site to work tirelessly as we pulled an all-nighter.

I was proud of the teamwork and the sense of coming together to do what was needed to get the job done. We had many laughs, shared a few buckets of Corona, and at 6:30 a.m., we were ready to meet with the production crew — only two hours before the start of the event. It was showtime and total chaos as I watched from behind the stage. This was a lesson in staying calm and trusting my team. It was a fast-paced, hectic day. Still, together, we turned frustrating moments into laughter and came away with a greater sense of purpose. We made sure to keep our spirits up with jokes and sarcasm. It was a brutal pace to keep up with the day's events, but we did have fun and got a ton of work done!

Equal Parts Fun and Hard Work

Maybe the secret recipe is equal parts of hard work and having fun. It's the approach that works best for me as a friend, a father, and a leader. We all define our kind of fun in different ways. I'm not talking about clowns and cotton candy. I choose to surround myself with positive people that I can count on to make my life more rewarding. This goes for my family members, close friends, and my employees. That's why I chose Craig, John, and Scott to work on my TLC leadership team. You know, if I was back in school and I got to pick my team for kickball, I would pick these same three guys.

The camaraderie that resonates between the four of us makes for a strong leadership team. We believe in the same vision: Changing people's lives. Those aren't just words. We work hard together to make TLC better for all Life Changers, customers, and our employees. As a dedicated team, we grow as leaders and learn from each other every day to operate at peak performance. Our brains seem to work better when we are in the right place with good people having a good time. Experiencing that sense of belonging to a team makes us enjoy coming into work.

I am grateful for their friendship, loyalty, and commitment to TLC. I have a special bond with these three guys. They embrace what makes me tick; my sense of humor, my singing, and my dumb jokes. The laughter naturally follows, and I wouldn't live any other way besides having fun, because we get more done.

Having fun, we get more work done.

The Derby Boys

Have

"To operate at your peak performance, you must have fun and be excited about what you do every day. Fun can be a catalyst for new ideas and problem-solving. To get more work done, you better be having some fun!"

Fun

CHAPTER 7
Give More

More. Sure, it's always easier to want more, but I believe in giving more.

"If your actions inspire others to dream More, learn More, do More, and becoMe More, you are a leader."

- John Quincy Adams

<u>More.</u> Sure, it's always easier to want more, but I believe in giving more.

One of the reasons I want to share my story is that I feel it's a way to give of myself. By opening up, being vulnerable, and making a connection authentically, my hope is to inspire you to follow your dreams and achieve more in life. We can't be afraid to express our thoughts, feelings, and emotions. We must be willing to give more of ourselves. It's not always easy or comfortable, but through these exchanges of open and honest communication are the times we grow as well as learn more about ourselves and the people we care about.

Everyone who knows me well, probably thinks my favorite word is "more". That's why the John Quincy Adams quote resonates with me; his words give meaning to my journey. It reminds me that it wasn't a single thing or one person that helped me to become a leader. Instead, it was my strong desire to become more, combined with the support and guidance of others, that truly made the difference.

Dave encouraged me to dream more.

Mike and Tony taught me to learn more.

Jenny believed in me to do more.

It's a cumulation of all these things that inspire me to give more.

From reading my story, you can see that my life is deeply rooted in my values. I have many special people and experiences to thank for that, starting with my granny, for teaching me about gratitude. When you start with a grateful mindset, it's easier to want to give more. I have learned throughout my life that even though our world has become a take-more society, it is far more rewarding when I give more than what's expected.

Stay True To Your Beliefs

At 47, I strive to live by my values every day, and while they are not unique to me, they define me. As a result, I feel a deeper connection with people, and I have more peace and contentment. Even through adversity, I do not waver.

Embracing the love on stage

We evolve as people based on who we spend our time with, the things we do, and the choices we make. That's why I believe we should stay true to our core values. By staying true to my own beliefs, it was only natural that my personal values would become the pillars for my company.

The truth about my vision: As a leader, I have always struggled to find the right words to communicate it in a way that everyone will easily understand and believe in as much as I do. Remember, Johnny told me it wasn't until his heart bought in that he truly made the connection? While thinking about this last core value, "Our standard is giving more than what's expected," is when the lightbulb came on in my head. I realized the easiest way to explain my vision is to make it relatable to this final core value. When I substitute the two words, "My vision" in place of "Our standard," everything becomes crystal clear.

"My vision" is giving more than what's expected.

It's not a secret. From the start, my vision has always been to give more by being a caring company and helping people change their lives. I understand that giving more means something different to everyone, and you may have your own words to describe it.

However, the words that come to my mind to best describe my vision include:

BELIEF

BELONGING

ENERGY

FAMILY

FRIENDSHIP

FUN

HEALTH

JOB...

...LOVE

MONEY

PATIENCE

RESPECT

SECURITY

SUPPORT

TIME.

This list could be much longer, but it's important to me that you see how these things create my vision of changing people's lives. Let's take one word on the list: Health; for example, we can further define it as mental, physical, emotional, spiritual, or financial.

Given this one word, my vision can impact someone in many ways. The most wonderful part is the ability to help people based on their unique needs.

Let your mind wander for a moment to think about what it would be like if we continually focused on helping people, not things, not money, not status.

In 1999, I chose to focus TLC's product line on health and wellness because it was a proven industry for sales success, but it's never been about money. My priority has always been focused on what I can do to transform someone's life. I value respect far more than money, and I don't run TLC to focus on Return on Investment; my focus is on Smiles on Investment. Like we say at TLC, "Health followed by wealth." There are days now that we seem less like a company and more like a group of people operating on a higher frequency energy.

My Addiction

As I travel around the world meeting new people, I have been asked numerous times what keeps me going. The answer is simple: It's in my DNA to help others. If you dig deep inside yourself to find your passion and uncover your gifts, you will never run out of energy, and you will naturally do more. There is no doubt that I am addicted to helping people; my vision goes well beyond selling health products. I'm committed to my passion, which gives me such a deep feeling of satisfaction that sometimes it feels like a spiritual awakening. When I give more, I continually have more.

Why do we put limits on ourselves and then impose them on those around us? When I allowed myself to dream, without limits, I found my true passion. I became empowered to break off the benefit handcuff and leave my job at the factory. What motivates me is seeing other people succeed, and I encourage you to open your mind and realize your potential. Allow yourself to dream without limits. Find your passion and be free to share your dreams and ideas with others. When you begin to push yourself in every aspect of your life, you will know you don't have to settle for less. Could it be the only person who is holding you back from doing more, is you?

God. Family. TLC.

There is nothing more powerful than prayer and human connection. I've met people from all walks of life with varying circumstances, lifestyles, and health issues. In our society, most people struggle at some point in life, either emotionally, physically, or financially, sometimes all at the same time. I know that being spiritual and having a strong family unit has helped me have a sense of balance and belonging.

I like to set aside time to pray every day, and I pray boldly and specifically. When we believe in God's plan, we stop looking at the past with regrets or being fearful of what the future holds. If you keep the faith, believe in yourself, and take the necessary steps to fulfill His unique plan for your life, you will see a shift in your mindset and behavior because you have put your trust in God.

" *Be true to yourself, help others, Make each day your Masterpiece, Make friendship a fine art, drink deeply from good books - especially the Bible, build a shelter against a rainy day, give thanks for your blessings and pray for guidance every day.* "

- John Wooden

The world is full of blame and anger, two of the most unproductive actions. If I feel disappointed about a situation or a setback, I don't get mad; instead, I pray and meditate to clear my mind of added noise, and then focus on something positive. I refocus by reading, working out, and of course, spending time with my greatest source of happiness, Jenny and our boys. It's also helpful for me to practice gratitude every day.

Keep Going. Don't Stop.

When I was young, I didn't think of myself as a leader, nor did anyone ever refer to me as a natural-born leader. Over the past 19 years since starting TLC, I have continually looked for the spark of inspiration for new ideas; when I come up with one new idea, 10 more follow. The spark is the reason I am always curious. Now, people call me an innovative leader, all because of my curiosity and being open to new ideas.

I like to be in a state of mental readiness, so I am an advocate of personal growth and professional development. I do not proclaim to know everything, but I do have an open mind to learn more every day. Many of the things that I have learned, I attribute to the people who chose to make me a priority and invest their time with me. Some of my most meaningful lessons are tied to experiences with family, friends, mentors, reading piles of books, and making mistakes and admitting them. Of course, there will be stressful moments, but I choose not to show negative energy or anger. I believe you have to push forward, or you fall back.

When was the last time you challenged yourself? Since the time I started working in my basement, I had to learn to trust myself to take some calculated risks and be confident that it was going to work out. It seemed like I made every mistake possible, but I didn't let that tarnish my vision.

There were plenty of setbacks and times when Jenny and I were broke, but it only ignited my entrepreneurial spirit, pushing me to keep the faith, work harder, and not give up.

I remind myself to focus on the goodness in people and the situation because I still believe that one person leads me to the next: Think about our Great Tea Shortage in 2015. When your life feels chaotic and everything seems to be going wrong, what would you do differently if you could hear me telling you every day, "Push, Push, Push!"? That's right, push yourself, and those around you, to do more. Look beyond your current circumstances, open your mind to new possibilities, refuse to give up, and most certainly do not let people or the past hold you back.

Most of us have walked on a treadmill before and know that you can choose to walk slowly with no incline or ramp it up and run. You can also choose an easy setting or go fast for endurance with interval training. Your decision may depend on how you feel that day or what results you are trying to achieve. Somedays, our choices may be based on how motivated we are to push ourselves to be physically fit. I use this workout analogy to convey a message about our approach to the work we do. We have choices; we can choose to casually walk through life or challenge ourselves to run a race filled with hills and valleys. How motivated are you?

There have been times since I started TLC, where I felt like I was sprinting through an obstacle course, fell, got up, kept running, and couldn't get to the finish line fast enough.

You have to put in the time, work hard, and go through a lot of ups and downs, like what we experienced in the basement, to truly appreciate your journey because the beauty comes from the life experiences that shape us and make us better. I say, bring on the mistakes and failures, so we can learn from them because where we are today with our success is because of where we have been with every mistake. If everything is easy, you will be disappointed when you reach your goal because obviously, it wasn't high enough. I like the saying; you have to go through the storm to get to the sun.

Loretta recieving " You're Amazing Award"

It's About Relationships

We see it all around us; people want a leader, mentor, maybe even a hero. We also crave a sense of belonging, to be understood, and acceptance. For me, it has never been products first; it's people first, the products are the tools to form connections and build relationships, and change people's lives. When we focus on transforming peoples' lives, the rest falls into place.

Our family, friends, co-workers, and even strangers come to us for a connection. It may be support, guidance, opportunity, love, or to belong to a caring community. Every one of us has the opportunity to provide people with a higher standard than what they expect. When we provide a standard they don't expect; they usually repay us with a standard that is more than we expect. I have experienced that people repay me with unique gifts such as friendship, loyalty, prayer, and gratitude. It's pretty magical when our lives are made richer by more valuable, intangible things that money can't buy.

We all know we can accomplish so much more when we have a strong team working together. Who would you pick for your kickball team? While I refer to playing kickball figuratively, it's about who you choose to surround yourself with now. Ask yourself, who has your back, no matter what? Who makes you better by working with them? That's what I love about network marketing; it's about building teams of support to achieve common goals.

One of the biggest things to consider when picking your team is, do you all have the same positive mindset and shared common goals? Like Johnny, Scott, Craig, and me. It's important to talk about your vision every day and continually preach where you are going. Make your passion known and understood to everyone you know and new people you meet. Find what motivates you, be determined, put in the hard work, and stay focused. Don't get too comfortable as it will hold you back, like my own experience of staying in the basement for two years too long.

Take time to listen and collaborate. I have learned along the way that so many good things come to us when we are willing to listen to other people's ideas and dreams. And by the way, as adults, I think we should all take time to play kickball with our employees and our kids. It's a great way to have more fun, but also to plant the seed in their minds of teamwork and collaboration.

I have a high-level focus on what I want, not the details. I think this may come from what Granny told me when I was young, "Jack, be happy, and remember that everything else is just details." I lead in a way that allows my employees to take the initiative to get things done as they see fit and determine what's best for the company. I trust my employees to make decisions that will help us to deliver the best service and products. We know that being a leader isn't always about managing people; it's about motivating them to be their best. At company meetings, my employees have heard me say, "The man who surrounds himself with the best is here to tell you that we can achieve anything if we work as a team. When you have the right people, it doesn't feel like work."

My Work Motto: Treat people better, and offer better products at better prices.

When We Dream, Amazing Things Happen.

Thinking back to the late nights when Jenny brought me dinner in the basement, and I was consumed with telling her my dreams, it was her support that made me feel like I could do anything. If I had not allowed myself to dream of more for my career and my family, I would have spent my life working on the assembly line.

Remember the day Rosa started working with Johnny and me in the basement? I asked her if she was ready to travel the world. Well, amazing things have happened since then. We are now operating in 17 countries and shipping TLC products to people in over 150 countries. In January 2020, the three of us traveled together to Russia to begin changing people's lives there. This trip reinforced my belief that there are no limits to what we can achieve if we work together with a common goal.

One Big Team

Network marketing is an emotional business because it's about people. Our sales representatives are called Life Changers because they are truly the catalyst for change. Our TLC battle cry is that no one can take better care of you or treat you better than we do. We put in a lot of hours and work hard every day to make sure our families feel loved, our customers are healthier, and our employees are appreciated. We make sure that our Life Changers feel supported and inspired to help people make total life changes. Generosity is at the heart of TLC, and we will always give more and never expect anything in return.

Inspired to change lives

There is an undeniable energy that comes from helping people to believe in themselves, have a better job, improved health, and financial security. That's why I give the same opportunity to everyone because I see the potential in people, even when they don't see it in themselves. The level of commitment that many of the Life Changers demonstrate is beyond my wildest dreams. They also give without expecting anything in return. Having a shared mindset is a powerful thing, and the fact that each person is unique and builds differently is what makes it extra special.

I am thrilled that we have over 100,000 Life Changers around the world who are committed to caring the most and sharing their stories to help others change their lives. We have heard countless testimonials from people all over the world who have had life-changing experiences as a result of being part of the TLC family. We have seen everything from improved physical health as a result of weight loss or reduced pain to other people who were struggling financially now having a better lifestyle.

Everyone can agree that a great business opportunity isn't just about having great products; it's so much more when you combine exceptional products with a true sense of belonging that stands for something greater. What's exciting to think about is that most Life Changers are with us because of the positive, personal connection they feel to be part of something bigger.

Thanks to the commitment of our Life Changers, there are days that it feels more like I have started a crusade than a business. TLC has become a place where people feel a deep sense of belonging, like a family, a sports team, a rock band, and raving fans. Some people even say we are a church for the non-church goers.

Engage. Encourage. Celebrate.

Another thing that makes TLC special is the diversity of our employees and Life Changers. We get a lot of recognition as a group of people who are loud, lively, and unstoppable. I encourage people to be exactly who they are because I don't believe in guilt or shame about anything or anyone in the room. We owe it to ourselves to provide unconditional support and encouragement to those around us. When we lift each other up, we all rise to unlimited levels.

When we lift each other up, we all rise to unlimited levels.

We are a meeting company, and the energy of TLC is contagious. The monthly events are a lot of work, like planning a huge wedding. Still, I believe the intimacy of each event, as well as the passion and excitement, is essential for the Life Changers and our employees. When I hear the testimonials of health and success, it is a serious jolt of believability. It's all worth it when I can sense the energy in the room, hear their laughter, and see their joy. It's incredible to witness the engagement of everyone coming together to celebrate as one big team reinforcing how much people need and value it.

At every TLC event, the leadership team stands in a circle holding hands and begins with prayer. I remind everyone that we must be present and in the moment. It's important to celebrate being together because everything goes so fast, and that's just life. We must not take people in our lives for granted. We are built with over 150 colorful cultures, and we need to be respectful when there are different views and beliefs. It is about compromise and shared life experiences that make us all better individually and collectively. When we come together to work to change lives around the world, you can feel it, and you know you are exactly where you are supposed to be.

Believe In More

When the world says you are not supposed to succeed, I don't believe it! I will believe in you even when you don't believe in yourself. I like to keep opening doors to do what is needed and give people a chance who haven't had one.

When I read the book, *The Moses Code* by James F. Twyman, I was inspired by these words: "It's time to realign your vision of yourself with the vision of God, who sees you as perfect and whole regardless of what you've done in the past. God's love is unconditional, and there's nothing you can do to interrupt it."

What's your vision?

To the TLC Life Changers: I hope to leave a lasting legacy that will inspire you to make an impact on the world. When my vision became about helping other people, it made all of my work so much easier and rewarding. Thank you for your belief in me and for providing others with a sense of belonging, faith, and a purpose to serve the greater good. Together, we will continue to change lives by connecting with people that believe in the same vision. Today, I pass the torch to you as a symbol of hope and solidarity to pass on to future generations.

Some final thoughts for you to consider. What will you do to make an impact on the world? Will you start by giving more than what's expected? My challenge for you is to keep pushing forward because when you think you are done, you've only begun.

Our Standard is Giving More Than What's Expected.

Give

"Don't give to get in return. When you can effectively give more than what's expected, others will be inspired to do the same. This standard generates a culture of pride, happiness, and fulfillment."

GOD. FAMILY. *TLC.*

I believe in God. I pray and put my faith in Him. Every day, I make Him my point of focus to ensure that I follow the path that He has planned for my life.

I am grateful to everyone whom I have ever met. Each person has taught me valuable life lessons. As a result, these lessons have helped me to become a better person, husband, father, friend, and leader.

My heart is full of gratitude when I think of my family. I'm blessed by their unconditional love and support of my dreams. A special shout out to my four sons for making my life better. When I hear you tell me you love me, it makes me feel like the luckiest father in the world.

Thanks to my friends for sticking by me throughout the years. You have made my life more fun and meaningful by the experiences we have shared.

I want to recognize all (past and present) TLC employees and Life Changers. It is because of your loyalty and dedication that we have grown to become a successful, worldwide direct sales company. Our future success depends on your continued commitment.

Lastly, I need to acknowledge our manufacturers. The employees at these companies have worked tirelessly to develop, test, and produce the best products that deserve to have the TLC label.

Believe in more! Together, we are changing people's lives.